Contents

Where is the United Kingdom?

Here is a map of the United Kingdom (UK).
The UK is in Europe.

North Atlantic Ocean

Aberdeen

SCOTLAND

EUROPE

Edinburgh
Glasgow

NORTHERN IRELAND

Belfast

UNITED KINGDOM

North Sea

IRELAND

Irish Sea

Leeds
Manchester
Liverpool

River Trent

River Severn

Birmingham

WALES

ENGLAND

NETHERLANDS

Cardiff

River Thames

London

BELGIUM

English Channel

FRANCE

There are four countries in the UK. They are Wales, Scotland, England and Northern Ireland.

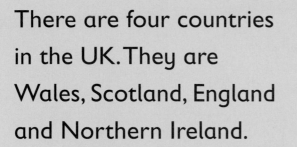

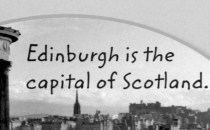

Edinburgh is the capital of Scotland.

London is the capital of England.

Cardiff is the capital of Wales.

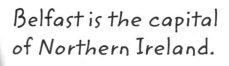

Belfast is the capital of Northern Ireland.

5

Land and sea

The UK has many different types of land. There are grassy hills, forests and marshes. Parts of the UK have lots of mountains.

Snow covers the top of Ben Nevis mountain in Scotland.

Ben Nevis is the highest mountain in the UK.

The UK has sea all around it. England, Wales and Scotland are on one island. Northern Ireland is on a different island.

The Giant's Causeway is a famous rocky area on the coast of Northern Ireland.

The weather

The weather in the UK is mild. This means it is not very hot or very cold. There are four seasons. These are spring, summer, autumn and winter.

People visit beaches and swim in the sea in the summer.

The south of the UK is warmer
and drier than the north. It can
rain at any time of the year.
It sometimes snows in winter.

Sometimes it rains so much that
rivers overflow and towns are flooded.

Town and country

Most people in the UK live in towns and cities. Some of the biggest cities are Birmingham, Manchester and Glasgow. London is the third largest city in Europe.

Around 8 million people live in London.

The Houses of Parliament are beside the River Thames in London.

Big Ben

Three quarters of all land in the UK is used for farming. Farmers grow crops such as wheat and potatoes. Cows and sheep live in grass fields.

Farmers use tractors to travel on their land and to harvest crops.

 # Homes

People in towns and cities often live in blocks of flats. Some of these buildings have many floors, and are very tall. Hundreds of people can live in one building.

These blocks of flats in Glasgow have 24 floors!

Many families in the UK live in terraced houses. A terraced house is joined to two other houses. The houses make a row along the street.

These terraced houses in England are around 100 years old.

🇬🇧 Shopping

People come to farmers' markets to buy food that is grown or made on nearby farms. Farmers sell fruit and vegetables, cheese, sausages and other products.

This stall has broccoli, red peppers and cucumbers for sale.

There are more than 550 farmers' markets in the UK.

cucumbers

broccoli

red peppers

Bunch of Beet...

The UK has many shopping centres. People can buy clothes, electronics, furniture and lots of other things in these centres.

Many tourists visit the Bullring shopping centre in Birmingham.

15

 # Food

Fish and chips is a very popular meal in the UK. The fish is coated in batter, a mixture of flour and water, and fried in oil. The chips are pieces of potato fried in oil.

Fish and chips is sometimes eaten with mushy peas. These are very soft cooked peas.

Different parts of the UK have special types of cakes and biscuits.

The Victoria sponge is a traditional English cake. It has cream and raspberry jam in the middle.

Shortbread is often eaten in Scotland. It is made with lots of butter, and it is very crumbly.

Welsh cakes are made with raisins and currants, and covered with sugar.

 # Sport

Rugby is a popular sport in the UK. It was first played 200 years ago at a school in England. Players can kick the rugby ball or run with it in their hands.

The other team has to get the ball off the player before he scores a try.

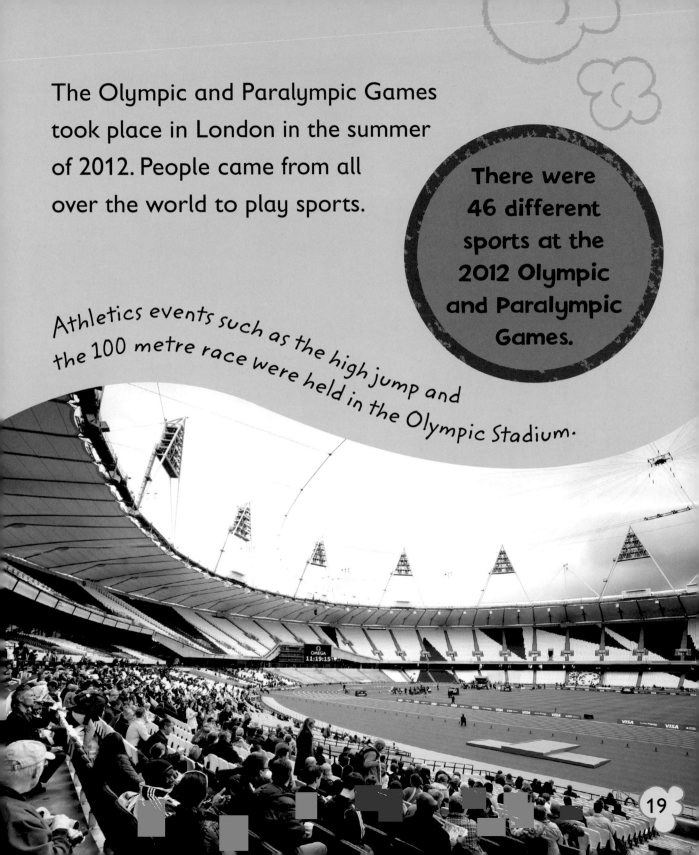

The Olympic and Paralympic Games took place in London in the summer of 2012. People came from all over the world to play sports.

There were 46 different sports at the 2012 Olympic and Paralympic Games.

Athletics events such as the high jump and the 100 metre race were held in the Olympic Stadium.

Holidays and festivals

On 5 November each year, people in the UK celebrate Bonfire Night. People watch fireworks, stand around large outdoor fires and light sparklers.

If you're very careful with sparklers, it can be a lot of fun to make patterns in the air with them!

May Day is celebrated on the first Monday of May. It is a national holiday. Some people perform traditional dances, such as maypole dancing.

Children hold on to long ribbons and dance around the maypole.

Flags of the UK

The flag of the United Kingdom is often called the Union Jack. Three of the countries in the United Kingdom also have their own flags. These countries are Scotland, Wales and England.

Try to match up each flag with the right part of the UK (or the whole of the UK, for the Union Jack).

1) Wales   2) Scotland   3) United Kingdom   4) England

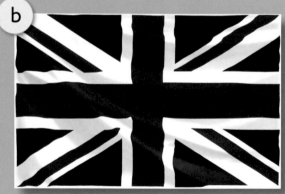

Bake yummy scones

You will need:
- 55g/2oz butter
- 25g/1oz caster sugar
- 1. 225g/8oz self-raising flour
- pinch of salt • 150ml/5fl oz milk
- 1 egg, beaten • large bowl
- pastry brush • pastry cutter

A scone is a small, round, biscuit-like cake. Most people think that scones were first made in Scotland, more than 500 years ago.

1. Ask an adult to turn on the oven to 220C/425F/Gas 7. In a large bowl, use your fingers to rub the butter into the flour and salt. Add the sugar and milk and make a ball of soft dough.

2. Place the dough on a flat surface. Use your hands to flatten it into a round shape that is 2cm (3/4 inch) thick. Cut out smaller circles with the cutter. Put them on a baking tray and brush their tops with beaten egg.

3. Ask an adult to put the scones in the oven. Bake for 12–15 minutes. Leave them to cool, and then spread with butter and jam. Yum!

Glossary

capital the city where the government of the country meets

crops plants grown on a farm

crumbly when something easily falls apart into small pieces

currants small dried fruits similar to raisins

flooded covered with water

harvest when a farmer's crops are fully grown, and are gathered to be eaten or sold

marsh grassy land that is often flooded with water

national holiday a day when most people in a country do not have to work or go to school

traditional something that has been part of a culture for a long time

try players score a try in rugby by touching the ball on the ground in a certain area

wheat a plant, part of which is used to make flour

Index